Everyday Heroes

Paramedics

Nichol Bryan
ABDO Publishing Company

visit us at
www.abdopub.com

Published by ABDO Publishing Company, 4940 Viking Drive, Edina, Minnesota 55435.
Copyright © 2003 by Abdo Consulting Group, Inc. International copyrights reserved in all
countries. No part of this book may be reproduced in any form without written permission from
the publisher.

Printed in the United States.

Editors: Kate A. Conley, Kristy Langanki Cannon, Kristianne Vieregger
Photo Credits: Corbis, TimePix
Art Direction: Neil Klinepier

Library of Congress Cataloging-in-Publication Data

Bryan, Nichol, 1958-
   Paramedics / Nichol Bryan.
      p. cm. -- (Everyday heroes)
   Includes index.
   Summary: Describes the role, training, and duties of paramedics.
   ISBN 1-57765-856-6
   1. Emergency medical technicians--Juvenile literature. [1. Emergency medical technicians. 2.
Occupations.] I. Title. II. Everyday heroes (Edina, Minn.)

RC86.5 .B79 2002
610.69'53--dc21

                    2002025365

Contents

abdo 14.95

10-02

Who Are Paramedics?

If you ever save a life, people may call you a hero. But there are some heroes who save lives every day. They are called paramedics.

Paramedics are people who have special medical training. They are not doctors, but they can perform many of the same tasks. Paramedics stop people from bleeding, keep broken bones from worsening, and help people breathe. They even deliver babies!

Paramedics rush to emergencies in **ambulances**. At the scene, paramedics care for sick or injured patients. Then they rush the patients to the hospital. Many people are alive today because a team of paramedics helped them in time.

Paramedics have a difficult and sometimes risky job. But we can all feel better knowing that they are nearby when we need them.

Paramedics are heroes with exciting and challenging careers.

Early Paramedics

The army began the first **ambulance** service in the United States during the **Civil War**. After the war, some hospitals started using ambulances, too.

Early ambulances were carriages pulled by horses. Sometimes a doctor rode in the ambulance. But often the only person in the ambulance was the driver. Usually the driver had no medical training. For this reason, many patients died before they could reach the hospital.

In the twentieth century, special trucks took the place of carriages. The trucks saved some lives because they could get to the hospital faster. But still, most ambulance drivers were not medically trained.

During the **Korean War**, the U.S. Army used a new method to help wounded soldiers. They trained some soldiers to give emergency medical care on the battlefield. These soldiers were called medics.

Early Ambulances

1864

1888

1900

1918

Some medics were trained to jump out of airplanes with **parachutes**. This way, they could quickly get to injured soldiers in places that were hard to reach. The parachuting medics came to be known as paramedics.

Paramedics help wounded soldiers during the Korean War.

In the 1960s, the U.S. government was concerned that so many people were dying in car crashes. They thought people with paramedic skills could save the lives of those involved in crashes. So the government began Emergency Medical Services (EMS) to better train paramedics. Eventually, hospitals began hiring paramedics. Fire and police departments hired them, too

Today, nearly every town and city has paramedics. Most paramedics are funded by tax money. Many paramedics work for private **ambulance** firms. These firms are usually supported by the city or **county** where they operate.

Paramedics are important in every community.

A Paramedic's Duties

Paramedics usually work in teams. The team members work together to help the patient at the scene of an emergency.

When the paramedics arrive, they have three basic jobs. First, paramedics must find out what's wrong with the patient. Then, they must treat the patient immediately. Finally, when the patient's health is stable, paramedics take the patient to the hospital.

The paramedics put the patient into the **ambulance** and rush to the emergency room. One paramedic drives the ambulance. The other paramedic rides in back with the patient.

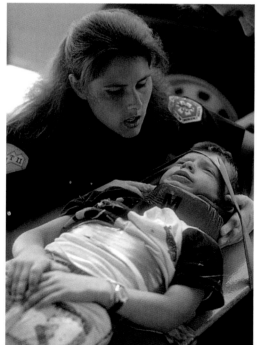

A paramedic takes care of a child who injured herself while bicycling.

At the hospital, the doctors and nurses take over caring for the patient. Sometimes during an emergency, paramedics communicate with the hospital by radio or computer. They tell the doctors what is wrong with the patient, and they find out what care to give.

Helping people involved in car accidents is an important part of being a paramedic.

Qualities of a Paramedic

What kind of person makes a good paramedic? Paramedics are people who enjoy helping others. They must be willing to work long hours and help at bad accidents. Often, paramedics put their own lives at risk to help others.

Paramedics must also stay calm during emergencies and **disasters**. Paramedics need to be strong and healthy, too. They must be able to lift patients onto cots and move big objects. Sometimes they must climb over obstacles to reach patients.

Good paramedics need to remember many facts and numbers. Paramedics must also have excellent communication skills. They need to calm other people in an emergency. They have to ask good questions to find out what's wrong.

Opposite page: Paramedics are proud
to help their communities.

Becoming a Paramedic

Each city and state has its own rules for becoming a paramedic. But in every state, paramedics must be at least 18 years old. They also must be high school graduates.

The training for paramedics can take up to two years. People who want to be paramedics take classes on emergency medical care. They also learn how to drive an **ambulance**.

After passing their classes, people who want to be paramedics take a written test. They must also show their lifesaving skills. For example, they show that they can perform **cardiopulmonary resuscitation (CPR)** and move a person with a back injury.

After passing these tests, paramedics get more training on the job. They go to emergencies and assist experienced paramedics. After completing this training, they can work as paramedics.

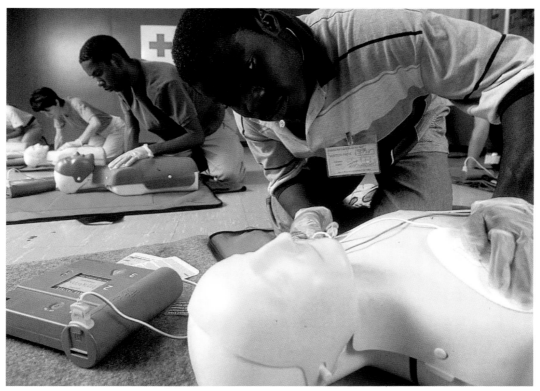

CPR is a skill that all paramedics must learn.

Paramedics continue learning throughout their careers. They take classes to learn new skills and to practice skills they already have. And they must pass the tests over and over again. In some states, paramedics must pass the tests every year.

Equipment

Paramedics are trained to use many types of equipment. They can use **electrocardiographs** and **defibrillators**. They can use backboards, which keep patients with back injuries from moving. They have **ambulance** cots to hold and move patients. They also have items such as bandages, blankets, and many different kinds of medicine.

Sometimes paramedics need to get patients out of a wrecked car or building before they can offer medical help. Paramedics can use saws to cut away the wreckage. They can also use the Jaws of Life. This powerful tool cuts metal, allowing paramedics to reach trapped patients.

Often, paramedics move patients to the hospital in an ambulance. Ambulances are specially made for the job they do. They carry much of the equipment that paramedics use to help patients.

Ambulances also have radios and computers. With this equipment, paramedics keep doctors informed. That way, the emergency doctors will be ready when the ambulance arrives at the hospital.

Paramedics also use **helicopters** to transport patients to the hospital quickly. Helicopters can land almost anywhere. They can fly over rough land and heavy traffic.

A paramedic checks to make sure his ambulance has all of the supplies needed for the next emergency.

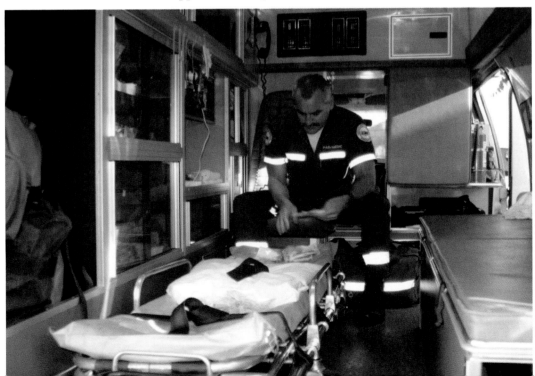

A Day's Work

Paramedics work long days. Often, they are **on call** 24 hours a day. Sometimes, they work three days and nights in a row. Then they get a few days off.

Paramedics can be busy when they are on call. One moment, they may rush to help victims of a fire. Later, they may help police officers control a violent criminal. Then they may assist an elderly person who has fallen at home.

Paramedics often must work in dangerous conditions. They may be called to rush into a burning building. They also may help people hurt by a natural **disaster**.

When they are not at an emergency, paramedics have other jobs to do. They clean and fix their equipment. They make sure their **ambulance** is well maintained. They also make sure they have all the supplies needed to handle any emergency.

Paramedics have difficult, dangerous jobs. But they enjoy their work. Paramedics like that every day is different. They feel good knowing that they save lives with their skills and fast action. They also like knowing that they make a difference.

Paramedics never know where the next call is going to take them.

Emergency Calls

Paramedics respond to many different kinds of emergencies. They may go to accidents, fires, crime scenes, or natural **disasters**. Paramedics help people who suffer from poisonings, heart attacks, allergic reactions, or **asthma** attacks. Sometimes paramedics need to stop a person from bleeding. They even deliver babies when the mothers can't make it to a hospital in time.

Paramedics use many skills and tools to determine what is wrong with a patient. Often, paramedics have just a few seconds to discover the problem. They do this by questioning the patient and other people at the scene. They also try to keep everyone calm.

Paramedics give the patient medical care right away. They use tools such as a **stethoscope** to listen to a patient's heart. Paramedics also use advanced tools such as an **electrocardiograph** to see how the patient's heart is working.

If paramedics discover the patient's heart and lungs have stopped working, they might need to give **CPR**. In CPR, the paramedic breathes into the patient's mouth to fill the lungs with air. She or he also pushes on the patient's chest to get the heart beating.

If the CPR is not successful, the paramedic might use a tool called a **defibrillator**. This tool has two paddles that put an electric shock in the patient's chest. The shock can help the heart beat normally again.

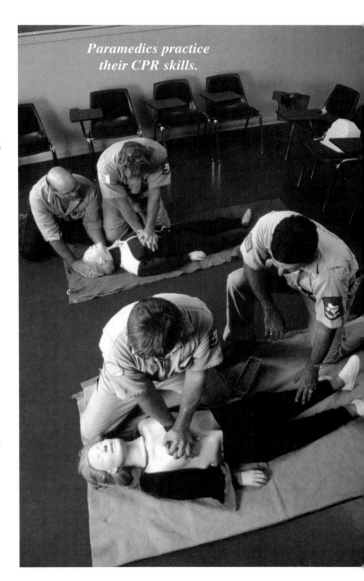
Paramedics practice their CPR skills.

Once the patient gets the most **urgent** care needed, the paramedics prepare the patient for the ride to the hospital. Sometimes the patient has broken bones or a bad back injury. In those cases, paramedics need to use **splints** or backboards to prevent further injury.

Once the patient is stable, paramedics put him or her into the **ambulance**. Then they drive the patient to the hospital. Driving the ambulance requires great skill.

Ambulance drivers must follow driving rules for emergency **vehicles**. They may drive much faster than the speed limit. They may go through stop signs or red lights without stopping. But they have to be careful. They don't want to hurt anyone!

Once at the hospital, the paramedics bring the patient into the emergency room. Then the doctors and nurses take over. The paramedics talk to the doctors about the patient's condition. They also write a report. The report tells about the emergency and what the paramedics did to help.

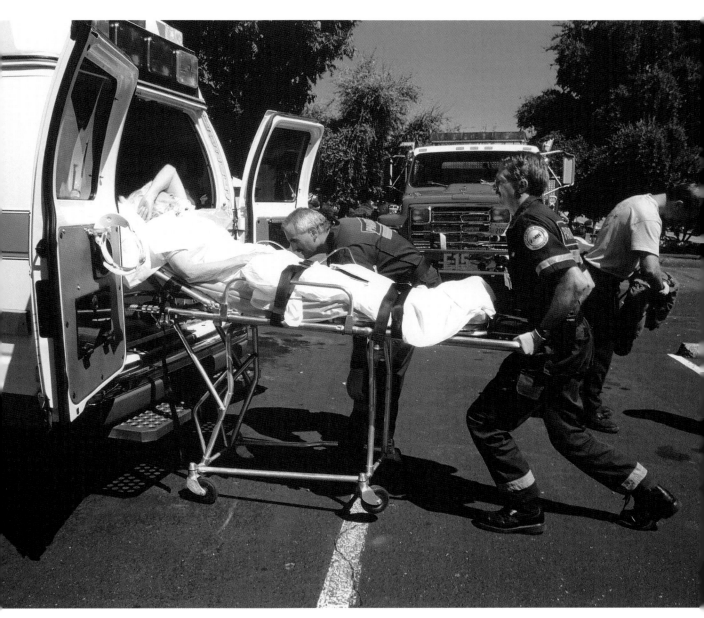

Paramedics place a patient into an ambulance.

Other Emergency Jobs

Paramedics have lots of people helping them. They are part of a group called **Emergency Medical Technicians (EMTs)**. There are different levels of EMT, ranging from an EMT-basic to a paramedic. The difference is how much medical training they have.

Paramedics also work with doctors and nurses at hospitals or in Mobile Intensive Care Units (MICUs). MICUs are special teams of doctors, nurses, and paramedics. They are trained to give advanced lifesaving care.

MICU paramedics go to the emergency in special **vehicles**. The paramedics use special equipment to communicate with MICU doctors and nurses. They give patients the same kind of care they would receive at the hospital.

Dispatchers provide another important emergency service. They help emergency service providers, such as police officers, firefighters, and hospital staffs. In most places, dialing 911 on the telephone connects the caller to an emergency dispatcher.

The dispatcher is often an **EMT**. He or she calms the caller and discovers the problem. Then the dispatcher sends the right kind of helpers to the scene. The dispatcher also tells the caller what to do for the patient before help arrives.

Dispatchers can help patients even before an ambulance arrives.

Paramedics & You

Besides helping in emergencies, paramedics provide other services for their communities. They work with hospitals to make sure their patients get good care. Paramedics teach public health courses, such as **CPR** and **first aid**. They work in their communities to prevent accidents and keep people healthy.

What if you have to call for the paramedics? Before an emergency happens, you should talk to your parents and teachers. They can teach you how and when to call for help. If you see an accident or an emergency, tell an adult right away.

EMTs often join with police officers and firefighters to help their community.

If there are no adults around, you may need to dial 911 or the emergency phone number for your area. When the dispatcher answers, remember that he or she is trained to help you. Answer the dispatcher's questions as best you can.

Remember, do not call 911 as a joke. Joke calls to 911 waste the dispatcher's time. Calling an emergency number for fun is a crime that could put someone's life at risk.

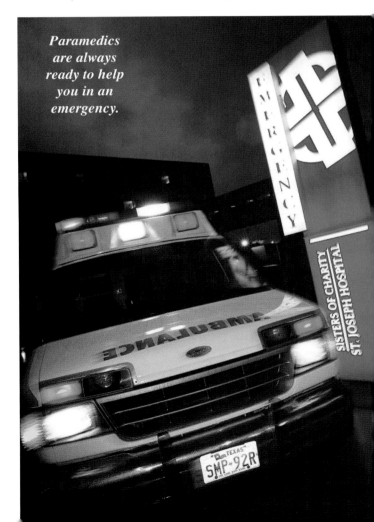

Paramedics are always ready to help you in an emergency.

Health & Safety Tips

By being careful, you can make sure no one has to call 911 for you. Learning how to stay safe is important for everyone. These are a few health and safety rules.

- Never try to light a match or lighter. If you find one, give it to an adult.
- Always wear a safety belt when you ride in a car. Safety belts keep you from getting hurt if the car is in an accident.
- Wear a helmet when you go biking, skateboarding, or in-line skating.
- Look both ways before you cross the street.
- Do not play with dogs or other animals you don't know.
- Stay with your friends when you play outside.
- Do not touch or drink anything with a poison symbol on it. That includes bottles or cans you may find under the sink, in the cupboard, or in the garage.
- Do not fly kites near high power lines. If the string touches the line, it could give you an electric shock.

To stay safe, wear a helmet when you go bicycling. A helmet can help protect you from head injuries if you have an accident.

Glossary

ambulance - a vehicle that carries sick or injured people.

asthma - a condition that makes breathing difficult and causes wheezing and coughing.

cardiopulmonary resuscitation (CPR) - an emergency lifesaving method in which someone tries to restart a patient's heart and lungs.

Civil War - a war between groups in the same country. The United States of America and the Confederate States of America fought a civil war from 1861 to 1865.

county - the largest local government within a state.

defibrillator - a tool used to restart or regulate a heartbeat.

disaster - an event that causes much sadness or loss.

electrocardiograph - an instrument used to see if the heart is working properly.

Emergency Medical Technician (EMT) - a person who is medically trained to assist patients at the scene of an emergency.

first aid - emergency care given to a person before regular medical care is available.

helicopter - an aircraft without wings that is lifted from the ground and kept in the air by horizontal propellers.

Korean War - 1950 to 1953. A war between North and South Korea. The U.S. government sent troops to help South Korea.

on call - to be ready to help at any time of the day or night.

parachute - a device used to safely jump out of an aircraft.

splint - a thin piece of hard material used to hold a broken bone in place.

stethoscope - an instrument used to listen to the sounds that the lungs and heart make.

urgent - demanding immediate action or attention.

vehicle - a car, truck, or bus.

Web Sites

Would you like to learn more about safety? Please visit **www.abdopub.com** to find up-to-date Web site links about the work that paramedics do to help other people and how you can stay safe, too. These links are routinely monitored and updated to provide the most current information available.

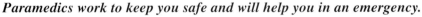

Paramedics work to keep you safe and will help you in an emergency.

Index